Message from the Director, NSA

The National Security Agency's rich legacy of cryptologic success serves not only as a reminder of our past triumphs, but also as an inspiration for our future.

Harry Truman, the man responsible for signing the legislation that brought our Agency into existence, was once quoted as saying, "There is nothing new in the world except the history you do not know." Like all truisms, it is only partially accurate. Each generation of Americans must at some point deal with unforeseen problems and issues that transcend the status quo. Most would agree that the challenges faced by NSA in today's war against terrorism are far different from those of World War II, Vietnam, or Desert Storm. Even so, President Truman was correct in his assertion that there is much to be learned from the past.

The history of the National Security Agency has in many respects been based on and characterized by feats of intellectual brilliance. Pioneers like William Friedman, Frank Rowlett, Dr. Louis Tordella, and Agnes Meyer Driscoll, to name but a few, were able to build on past successes and do whatever was necessary to meet the challenges of their time.

We should not forget, however, that NSA's success is due not just to the efforts of the well-known legends of the cryptologic past, but also to the dedicated work of thousands of men and women whose names will never be noted in any history book. History tells us that both genius and hard work are required to ensure success. Thankfully, as an Agency, we have been blessed with both in our past efforts to provide and protect America's most important information.

In conclusion, on the occasion of our golden anniversary, it is fitting and appropriate to remember and reflect on NSA's half-century of exemplary service to our nation. By increasing our knowledge of our storied past, we will hopefully gain the inspiration required to inspire us in the future. Even though NSA has done the Nation's work for 50 years, to paraphrase a Robert Frost poem, we "have promises to keep and miles to go before we sleep."

MICHAEL V. HAYDEN
Lieutenant General, USAF
Director, NSA/Chief CSS

Message from the Deputy Director, NSA

We have a rich legacy of success. For five decades, the information edge provided by the world's best cryptologic organization has played a substantial role in shaping our national enterprise. During the Cold War, NSA provided the transparency into the intentions of our adversaries and the secure communications needed to keep major power confrontations from escalating to nuclear conflict. In recent years it has provided an unprecedented battlefield advantage to U.S. forces in the Persian Gulf, the Balkans, and Afghanistan; helped shape the global security environment; and supported American diplomacy around the world.

These achievements are the product of 50 years of sustained innovation. From Morse code to cyberspace, generations of cryptologists have worked at the forward edge of technology and expanded the art of the possible. The Nation is in their debt.

Those who've worked at NSA one year or 40 are privileged to carry this work forward. As in the past, the need is great. As in the past, all depends on our ability as an organization to think our way past today's limits, transform our technology and ourselves, and keep the edge. Our 50th Anniversary isn't a milestone. It's a starting line.

WILLIAM B. BLACK, JR.
Deputy Director, NSA

National Security Agency
America's Codemakers and Codebreakers

The National Security Agency is the Nation's cryptologic organization. NSA creates decisive U.S. strategic and tactical advantage by providing otherwise denied information to U.S. decision makers while at the same

time denying access to U.S. information and information systems by America's adversaries. The ability to understand the secret communications of our foreign adversaries while protecting our own communications – a capability in which the United States leads the world – gives our Nation a unique advantage.

Signals Intelligence (SIGINT) and Information Assurance (IA) complement each other. SIGINT gives the Nation an information advantage over its adversaries. IA prevents others from gaining advantage over us. Together the two missions promote a single goal: information superiority for America and its allies.

Information Assurance

Today's complete reliance on critical information systems has fundamentally altered the Nation's requirements for information systems security. The need to protect vital information has become essential. By using the most sophisticated networked information systems in the world, U.S. leaders and military are able to gather, understand, and use information better and faster than any potential adversary. This is the information advantage that must be protected.

In the past, the Information Assurance Directorate of the National Security Agency produced "black

boxes," cryptographic gear that secured point-to-point communication links and paper keying material to be used with them. Simply, security equated to "confidentiality," and systems were not interconnected. But technology evolved, and so did services, as NSA moved from Communications Security (COMSEC), to Information Systems Security (INFOSEC), to Information Assurance (IA). The needs of today's world are different, and so is IA.

NSA protects information today with a mix of commercial and government solutions, based on a defense-in-depth strategy — multiple roadblocks between critical systems and the adversaries who would exploit them – layers of security technologies and services within an information device, system, or infrastructure. This approach enables customers to use those security layers that are appropriate for their particular risk management profile and budgetary constraints. No longer are they forced to adopt the "one-size-fits-all" model from the past.

This defense-in-depth strategy combines people, technology, and operations:

❖ **People** such as trained system administrators and users

❖ A **technology** program that leverages developments in the commercial world

❖ Active defensive information **operations** to detect intrusions into our systems and respond to them.

While we still need to guarantee confidentiality, today's IA is broader, encompassing five dimensions:

❖ Confidentiality - assurance against unauthorized or unintended disclosure

❖ Data integrity - assurance that data has not been modified

❖ User authentication - assurance that the legitimate party created or sent the data

❖ Transaction non-repudiation - assurance that the party cannot later deny it

❖ System availability - assurance of access to the data.

NSA faces a major challenge in helping its IA customers keep pace with advances in technology. It supports research and partners with industry to give customers products that are better in every way.

Signals Intelligence

NSA has the mission to collect, process, and disseminate Signals Intelligence (SIGINT) information for foreign intelligence and counterintelligence purposes consistent with applicable U.S. laws and with full consideration of the rights of U.S. persons. Foreign intelligence is defined as information relating to the capabilities, intentions, and activities of foreign powers, organizations, or persons. Counterintelligence is defined as information gathered and activities conducted to protect against espionage and other intelligence activities.

The SIGINT mission is to provide the Nation with intelligence to ensure national defense and to advance U.S. global interests by collecting, processing, and disseminating SIGINT information on foreign powers, organizations, or persons, and international terrorists. NSA collects, processes, and disseminates intelligence reports on foreign targets in response to information needs levied by all departments and levels of the United States Executive Branch to include the Department of Defense.

The SIGINT mission faces challenges in collecting, analyzing, and disseminating relevant, timely information for national policymakers and military commanders. In the information age, the volume of information grows daily, as does the velocity of change in telecommunications technologies and variety of means to transmit and store voice, data, and video.

The relatively static Cold War environment has been replaced by an ever-changing telecommunications environment. Likewise, customer requirements and priorities shift rapidly in response to information needs related to foreign political, economic, military, and information needs. NSA targets' use of modern telecommunications technology continues to pose significant challenges to NSA in the ways that communications are transmitted, to include the use of encryption. Likewise, target use of various languages and telecommunications applications requires NSA to maintain a wide variety of capabilities.

To meet the challenges of the information age – its volume, variety, and velocity – NSA has embarked on a transformation path to ensure we have the right capability at the right time to meet the information needs of our customers. Transformation in people, systems, business processes, and use of technology will allow NSA to meet the challenges of the future.

NSA plays a key role in national security by employing people, technology, and operations to provide America's leaders with the critical information they need to save lives, defend democracy, and promote American values while protecting vital information through "cryptologic excellence — yesterday, today and tomorrow."

"When the fate of a nation and the lives of its soldiers are at stake, gentlemen do read each other's mail -- if they can get their hands on it."

Allen Dulles,
The Craft of
Intelligence, 1963

In the beginning, people whispered. Others eavesdropped. And from these humble caveman origins have evolved one of the most powerful forms of intelligence and one of the most important forms of security in the world today.

All of this has come about largely because communication has grown from person-to-person talk to satellite to Internet. This growth has provided even greater opportunities to gather information about what enemies, present and potential, are planning — information that has determined the fate of people and nations. A solved dispatch revealing German plans to join forces with Mexico in invading the United States so enraged America that it declared war on Germany in 1917, with all that has entailed. More recently, these new forms of communications and even new kinds of cryptography make it possible to transact business deals with the speed of light and with complete confidence in their security.

The National Security Agency deals with these matters. It solves messages of hostile powers and organizations, and it helps keep American military and civil messages secure. It is not the only means of keeping Americans safe, but it is an important one.

DAVID KAHN
Author of <u>The Codebreakers</u>

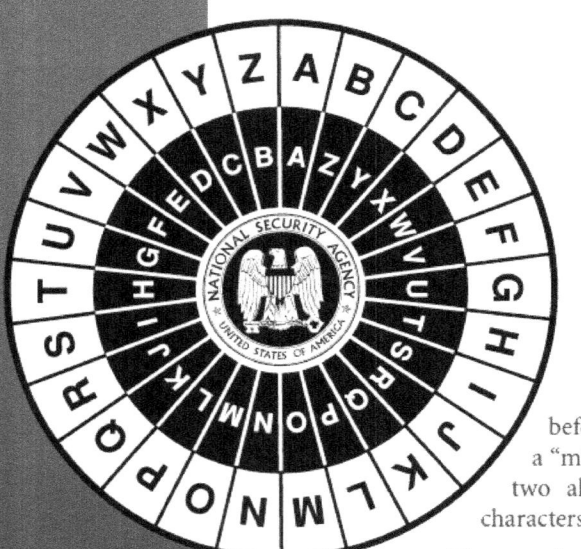

The cipher disk has a distinguished history. As invented in Italy sometime before 1470, it had similar concentric disks with the exception that one contained a "mixed" (scrambled) alphabet. Also, in some of the earlier versions, one of the two alphabets was composed of arbitrary symbols in lieu of conventional characters.

The appeal of the disk lay in the fact that with it, encipherment and decipherment could be performed without carrying bulky or compromising written materials.

The cipher disk came into large-scale use in the United States for the first time in the Civil War. The Federals' chief signal officer patented a version of it, very similar to the Italian disk, for use in flag signaling. Since his flag stations were often within the view of Confederate signalmen, he prescribed frequent changes of setting.

About half a century later, the U.S. Army adopted a simplified version in which one alphabet was "standard" and the other "reverse-standard." Although technically this was a step backward, there were compensating advantages since the regularity of the alphabets tended to reduce error. During World War I and for several years after, the Army issued the disk in this form to units that needed a cipher that could be carried and used easily and that would give a few hours' protection to tactical messages.

In terms of using this device, the two disks could be left in the same setting for an entire message, producing the simplest possible cryptogram, or their setting could be changed with every letter of the message. If the pattern of the settings were complex enough, an extremely secure cipher would result.

The Beginnings

Cryptology was of service to Americans even before the United States itself was born. During the Revolutionary period, American patriots often used ciphers to protect their communications. Occasionally during the Revolutionary War, encrypted British messages fell into American hands, and military officers, as well as several members of the Continental Congress, were called upon to solve them.

In the American Civil War, the Industrial Revolution first became a close partner with warfare. Armies moved rapidly over rail, and communications had to keep up. Both the Union and the Confederacy depended on the newly invented telegraph to control their armies in distant theaters of war. Both sides adopted visual signal systems for field operations based on waving a single flag. Both types of communications were vulnerable to intercept, which put a premium on encryption to protect friendly messages and on cryptanalysis to read the enemy's signals. Neither side had cipher systems that could withstand a concerted attack, and this new "communications intelligence" became a major source of information in Washington, Richmond, and many far-flung battlefields. In the long period of peace that followed the Civil War, the U.S. State Department and the military used codes or ciphers to protect sensitive communications, but the government did not conduct any organized cryptanalytic activities.

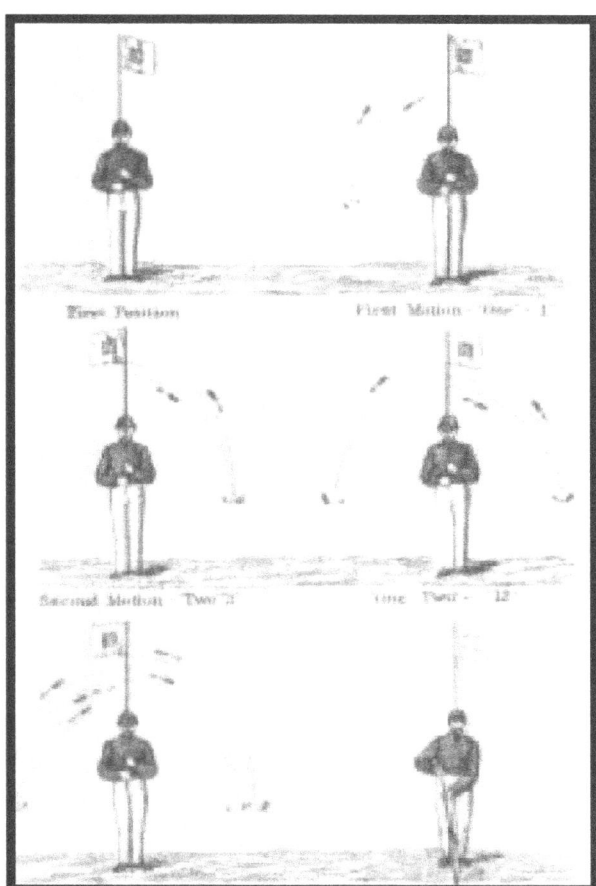

Union soldiers during the first two years of the Civil War relied entirely on the "wig-wag" system for communications

George Washington had a keen appreciation for the need for intelligence, and it is well known today that he was skillful in using spies to gather data on British forces. He worried about the security of his spies and concerned himself with ciphers for espionage use. He also employed cryptanalysis in the famous case of Dr. Benjamin Church, a Boston physician and Washington's director general of hospitals. Church was caught sending an enciphered message across the lines. Washington enlisted the aid of Elbridge Gerry (later vice president of the United States) and the Reverend Samuel West. Both broke the cipher, which cloaked a report to a British general about American military plans and capabilities. Church was imprisoned.

"It may well be doubted whether human ingenuity can construct an enigma of the kind which human ingenuity may not, by proper application, resolve."

Edgar Allan Poe, from the "The Gold Bug"

World War I

The invention of wireless radio at the turn of the century brought communications and cryptology into a new era. The new source, then termed "radio intelligence," was adopted by the U.S. Navy and the Army, and was first used operationally during the Mexican border incursion of 1916, when the Army pursued Pancho Villa into northern Mexico. The U.S. commander, General Pershing, took with him mobile intercept vans — then known as "radio tractors" — to listen to radio messages sent by Mexican government forces. This was the first mobile intercept station in American history; the use of these mobile units was later adopted by American forces when Pershing led U.S. forces to France in 1917. All the major combatants in World War I engaged in radio intercept — then known as "listening in" — and cryptanalysis of enemy messages.

Radio Tractor Unit
A communications intelligence mobile collection unit on the Mexican border, 1916

Pershing's forces, like virtually all the others, were well outfitted for radio intelligence work. Army-level support came from Section 8 of the new Army intelligence service. In France, battlefield communications intelligence support was conducted by an organization entitled G2A6, with intercept sites at fixed locations and "radio tractors" following the troops at the front lines.

An Army intercept station in France, 1918

In addition to their authorized codes, American Expeditionary Forces in Europe during World War I occasionally employed various unauthorized codes of varying degrees of security. One of the codes used by the 52nd Infantry Brigade was a typically American one:

Killed	Strike out
Seriously wounded	Base on balls
Slightly wounded	Hit by pitched ball
Have taken (no.) prisoners	Stolen bases (no.)
Have lost (no.) prisoners	Left on base (no.)
Fired on by machine guns	Johnson using fast ball
We were bombarded with gas	Wagner singled
We were under heavy bombardment	Wagner knocked a home run
Our artillery laid down a barrage	Sent in a pinch hitter
We bombarded heavily	Cobb knocked a home run
Commissioned officer	Majors
Enlisted men	Minors

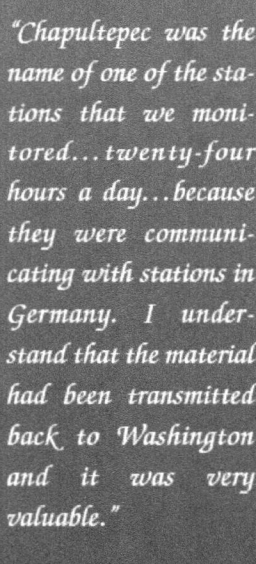

At the conclusion of World War I, building on the wartime MI-8, the United States for the first time established a peacetime cryptanalytic organization, which was directed by Herbert O. Yardley. Yardley had

been an important figure in the wartime operations against enemy encrypted communications. After the war, the State and War Departments continued the task, this time targeted against foreign diplomatic cable traffic; Yardley was chosen to lead the effort. His most famous success came in 1923 during the Washington Naval Conference, which was seeking ways to prevent a postwar arms race. Under MI-8, Yardley broke Japanese diplomatic messages and sent the information to the State Department, which in turn used it to negotiate favorable provisions in the final agreements. In 1930, however, a new Secretary of State, Henry Stimson, withdrew the State Department's funding from MI-8, causing its collapse. No longer in government service, Yardley wrote a "tell-all" book, *The American Black Chamber*, which publicized MI-8's achievements. Among other effects, it caused a number of countries to search for and adopt new encryption methods.

Herbert O. Yardley,
founder of MI-8, the "Black Chamber"

Examples of messages related to the Washington
Naval Conference decrypted and translated by
Yardley's MI-8

The Origins of Modern Services

With Yardley's "Black Chamber" closed, the Army turned to an existing code-making organization under William Friedman, the Signal Intelligence Service (SIS), to take on the job of both making and breaking codes. Friedman, arguably the leading cryptologist of his time, became known as the father of

SIS in the mid-1930s

modern Army cryptology. William Friedman's wife, Elizebeth, was his equal as a cryptologist. They met and married prior to World War I when both were employed at a private research foundation. After the war, William went into Army cryptography as a civilian consultant; Elizebeth went into the Coast Guard, where she founded its cryptologic effort. Her cryptanalytic efforts against rumrunners during Prohibition resulted in the incarceration of a number of criminals and brought her national recognition. In 1930, William Friedman hired the Army's first three civilian "junior cryptanalysts," all of whom gained their skills under his tutelage. These men, Frank Rowlett, Abraham Sinkov, and Solomon Kullback, later joined by Japanese translator John Hurt, formed the core of Army cryptologic work in the 1930s and became principal figures in American cryptology over the next three decades.

Coast Guard intercept/DF unit

William F. Friedman, the dean of modern American cryptologists, pioneered the application of scientific principles to cryptology and laid the foundation for present-day cryptologic concepts. Born in Kishinev, Russia, on September 24, 1891, he was brought to the United States in 1892. Following graduation from Cornell University in 1914 with a degree in genetics, he worked for Riverbank Laboratories, first as director of its Department of Genetics and then as director of the Department of Ciphers. After serving in World War I as a lieutenant with the American Expeditionary Forces, he became chief cryptographer of the Signal Corps, then Director of Communications Research, Signal Intelligence Service (later Army Security Agency). After the end of World War II, Mr. Friedman served in various positions, including cryptologic consultant to the Army Security Agency, the Armed Forces Security Agency, and the National Security Agency. For his many contributions to the security of his country, Mr. Friedman received the War Department Medal for Exceptional Civilian Service, the Presidential Medal for Merit, the Presidential National Security Medal, and a special congressional award of $100,000 for inventions and patents in cryptology. Mr. Friedman was the author of many books, brochures, technical treatises, and articles on cryptologic subjects. In addition, with his wife, Elizabeth Smith Friedman, he wrote *The Shakespearean Ciphers Examined*. Mr. Friedman died in Washington, D.C., on November 2, 1969.

Laurance Safford

Joseph Wenger

The Navy established a communications intelligence (COMINT) organization in 1924, initially with the mission of training cryptologists to be ready in case of war. Laurance Safford established the first Navy cryptologic organization, called the Research Desk, or OP-20-G, and led its activities for decades. Safford attracted many brilliant officers into the organization, including Joseph Wenger.

The enlisted men trained in intercept skills inside a wooden shed atop the Navy building in Washington, D.C.; thereafter, this exclusive group was known as the "On the Roof Gang." Friedman and his colleagues in SIS studied Japanese diplomatic machine-generated ciphers, the successor systems to those Yardley had been reading in the 1920s. SIS gave the highest level Japanese systems covernames from rainbow colors: RED, adopted in 1935, and PURPLE, adopted in 1939. These complicated ciphers were solved by mathematical analysis; the cryptanalysts never saw one of the original Japanese machines. In order to read PURPLE-based messages quickly enough, a young Army engineer named Leo Rosen designed an "analog" machine. Once the key to the message was broken, an operator could plug the machine into two typewriters, type the cipher text on one machine, and get plain text on the other. Designed by the Army, fabricated and partially funded by the Navy, the PURPLE was an early example of interservice cooperation in cryptology.

From about 1940, even before the United States entered World War II, the U.S. and Great Britain began cautious sharing of scientific and technical information; eventually, this included sharing of cryptologic information. The U.S. told the British of its successes against Japanese diplomatic ciphers and provided the British with a PURPLE analog; the British, in turn, informed the U.S. of their ability to read German military messages enciphered on the ENIGMA machine and gave the Americans access to decrypts of important messages. These initial steps led to increased cooperation in cryptanalysis once the United States became engaged in the war. Eventually, Americans were integrated into the operation at Bletchley Park, the wartime headquarters of the British cryptologic organization. Just as both nations drew closer in combat against their common enemies, they cooperated closely in solving and exploiting the communications of these enemy forces.

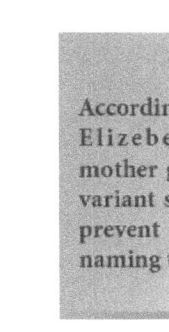

According to a family story, Elizebeth Friedman's mother gave her name this variant spelling in order to prevent anyone from nick-naming the child "Eliza."

Members of the "On the Roof Gang"

PURPLE Analog, the SIS-devised machine that read Japanese diplomatic messages beginning in 1940

Bletchley Park

9

The U.S. ability to exploit Japan's diplomatic communications in the early 1940s gave it a distinct advantage in the negotiations of that period. However, by 1941 U.S. Army and Navy cryptanalysts had not solved the military code systems used by the Japanese. Thus, despite high-quality secret information about Japan, the U.S. did not learn in advance that a Japanese Navy task force had been sent to bomb American installations on Hawaii. The Japanese attack at Pearl Harbor and other installations on December 7, 1941, propelled the United States into another world war. In the months immediately after the Pearl Harbor disaster, the U.S. Navy made important breakthroughs in a high-level Japanese Navy code known to the Americans as JN-25. The solution to this system enabled the U.S. to read Japanese planning and operational messages throughout the Pacific War. With this inside knowledge, the U.S. was able to position itself to turn back a Japanese naval thrust into the Coral Sea near Australia, and, in May 1942, handed the Japanese Navy a resounding defeat at the island of Midway.

Arlington Hall Station

In 1942, the Army's Signal Intelligence Service (SIS) moved from cramped quarters at the Munitions Building on the Mall in Washington, D.C., to a recently purchased girls' school in Arlington, Virginia, which became known as Arlington Hall Station (AHS). SIS's successes against Japanese code systems contributed to its rapid expansion from several people to several thousand. SIS supported operations against both Japanese and German communications. Much of the work at Arlington Hall was conducted by cleared personnel of the Women's Army Corps (WAC).

Naval Security Station

> General George S. Patton, the legendary commander of World War II, became an astute consumer of communications intelligence (COMINT); he learned its worth in the drive across Western Europe after D-Day and used it well. For example, in mid-August 1944, while Patton's Third Army was located near the French city of Le Mans, the general and about 40 of his officers attended daily intelligence briefings. Here they would hear regular briefings by the G-2 (Intelligence) and G-3 (Operations), situation reports, and a news report from radio broadcasts. Following each meeting, all but seven officers were dismissed, and the rest stayed for a briefing on the enemy situation as seen in COMINT. This source proved valuable for the Third Army: ULTRA (the codeword assigned to COMINT derived from decryption of high-level German ciphers) material alone predicted a drive by five German Panzer divisions against the Third Army at Avaranches. In another instance, when Third Army headquarters moved near Chalons, an ULTRA message arrived at 0100 hours showing the German order for an attack at 0300. Patton had described the U.S. troops in the attack areas as spread out as "thin as the skin on an egg." He found means to alert the defending divisions without jeopardizing the security of ULTRA, and the German attack was repulsed.
>
> One member of Patton's staff wrote about the value of ULTRA to Patton's army stating that, "An army has never moved as fast and as far as the Third Army in its drive across France, and ULTRA was invaluable every mile of the way."

"The intelligence which has emanated from you before and during this campaign has been of priceless value to me. It has simplified my task as commander enormously. It has saved thousands of British and American lives, and in no small way contributed to the speed with which the enemy was routed and eventually forced to surrender."

Dwight D. Eisenhower, 1945

Like SIS, the Navy's OP-20-G outgrew its quarters on the Mall in Washington, D.C., and in 1942 moved to a girls' school at Ward Circle (later known as the Naval Security Station) in a northwest corner of the District of Columbia. OP-20-G coordinated cryptologic operations in support of American fighting forces and cooperated with the British cryptologic organization, but did so in official channels separate from the Army.

In partnership with the British at Bletchley Park, the U.S. Navy mounted an effort against the German naval ENIGMA cipher machine. Naval cryptanalysts were able to read the enemy's most secret messages by using a device known as the Bombe. This four-rotor diagnostic machine, which had components that emulated the fixtures on the ENIGMA, was based on a British version, redesigned by the U.S. Navy and built by National Cash Register Corporation at Dayton, Ohio. Virtually the entire U.S. effort to solve ENIGMA codes was staffed by Navy WAVES — the headquarters of OP-20-G had employed over 5,000 women at the height of the war. The ability to read German ENIGMA-based naval messages was of vital importance in the war in the Atlantic, particularly against German submarines. American military forces in all theaters of war received cryptologic support from the central organizations and theater centers through special intelligence distribution arrangements. In addition, wartime brought rapid movement of forces, especially during the "Dash across France" in 1944. Army cryptologists supported the front-line troops by solving low-level codes and ciphers on the spot, the World War II version of the radio tractor unit.

Navy WAVE maintains the ENIGMA-cracking Bombe

During World War II, the United States had the best of both possible cryptologic worlds. In conjunction with their British ally, U.S. personnel had secret access to the wartime communications of enemy forces. At the same time, a joint Army-Navy project produced the best communications security device of World War II, the SIGABA. Of the major machine cipher systems of the wartime period, only the SIGABA, used for U.S. high-level communications, remained impenetrable to enemy cryptanalysis, a fact that was confirmed in postwar interrogations of German and Japanese cryptologists — it was the acme of wired rotor cryptography.

Of all forms of communications, the human voice has been the most difficult to encrypt successfully. At the beginning of World War II, after several abortive attempts, Bell Laboratories produced the SIGSALY. Although successful in encrypting speech, it had limited application because of its size: SIGSALY consisted of forty-five racks of equipment, weighed fifty-five tons, occupied an entire room, and required thirteen technicians to operate. At $1 million per copy, it was produced for only a few strategic command centers between the U.S. and Great Britain, notably between the White House and Winston Churchill's underground headquarters in London.

SIGSALY

On the front lines, both the U.S. Marine Corps and the U.S. Army used another very effective form of communications security: Native Americans speaking in a verbal code in their own languages to "encrypt" tactical voice communications. The Marines used Navajo "code talkers" exclusively, while the Army drew from the Comanche, Choctaw, Ojibwe, and Cherokee tribes.

Cryptology did not win the war. The war was won by the brave soldiers, sailors, airmen, and Marines who risked their lives in combat with the enemy. However, the ability to read the enemy's most secret messages allowed American and British commanders to make wise decisions about the use of their troops; this shortened the time of war and saved countless thousands of Allied lives. The ironclad protection of U.S. high-level communications prevented the enemy's intelligence personnel from exploiting these messages; this superior communications security effort also saved an untold number of lives and contributed greatly to the success of Allied operations.

An Army COMINT intercept truck in France, 1944

Code Talkers in the field

German soldiers using the ENIGMA in the field

Postwar Period

Despite the historic achievements of American cryptology during World War II, the Army and Navy emerged from the war as disunited rivals in the business. In 1947, the Air Force became a third competitor for funding, equipment, and personnel. At the same time, the technology of cryptology had become much more sophisticated through the use of powerful machines and rudimentary computers and, hence, much more expensive. Several forward-looking leaders recognized the necessity to merge the efforts of both services to attack increasingly sophisticated targets. Joseph Wenger, one of Laurance Safford's earliest recruits to OP-20-G, urged more cooperation with the Army. After several unsuccessful attempts to achieve economy and compatibility of operations through plans for coordination, in 1949 the Secretary of Defense established a central cryptologic institution, the Armed Forces Security Agency (AFSA). Under the Joint Chiefs of Staff, AFSA was intended to be the unifying organization, but it lacked the enforcement powers to make it dominant. What resulted from good intentions was yet a fourth cryptologic contender, which had to compete with the other three service agencies for resources.

Army Security Agency mobile direction finding unit in Korea

AFSA's considerable technical successes were overshadowed by its failure to truly unite the Service Cryptologic Agencies. The Korean War of 1950-53 exposed a number of serious weaknesses in the postwar cryptologic community. While there was SIGINT support from AFSA and first-class support on the front lines, senior commanders were dissatisfied because this support never approached the level they had enjoyed during World War II. In addition, even this limited war in Korea exposed continuing problems in service cryptologic cooperation and areas of duplication of effort. At the same time, some of the civilian arms of the government, particularly the State Department and the CIA, were dissatisfied with the strong military character of the U.S. SIGINT effort. With both military and civilian leaders dissatisfied, albeit on different points, it became clear to senior members of the U.S. government that changes in cryptologic organization had to be made. President Harry S. Truman commissioned a study in 1952.

ASA was responsible for supplying the Army's codes and ciphers. Here a soldier of the 3rd Infantry Division uses the World War II vintage M-209 cipher device in his foxhole message center.

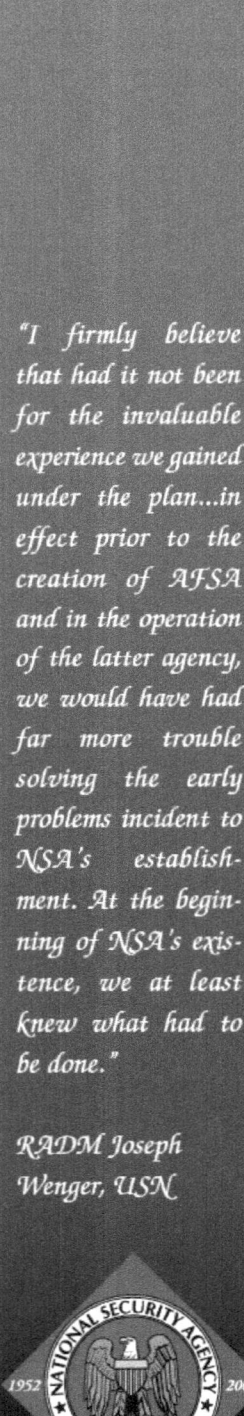

"I firmly believe that had it not been for the invaluable experience we gained under the plan...in effect prior to the creation of AFSA and in the operation of the latter agency, we would have had far more trouble solving the early problems incident to NSA's establishment. At the beginning of NSA's existence, we at least knew what had to be done."

RADM Joseph Wenger, USN

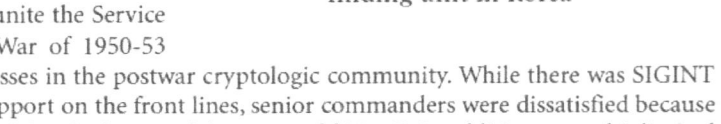

The Creation of NSA

President Harry Truman signed the memorandum that created the National Security Agency in 1952

NSA's new headquarters, 1957

President Truman in 1952 impaneled a high-level committee chaired by George Brownell, a New York lawyer, after hearing reports from the director of the Central Intelligence Agency, Walter Bedell Smith, and the Secretary of State, Dean Acheson, that AFSA was not working. The Brownell Committee, concluding that cryptology was a "national asset," recommended that cryptology be taken from control of the Joint Chiefs of Staff and resubordinated to the Secretary of Defense. The Secretary was made the Executive Agent for SIGINT for the government. Truman established NSA with nothing more than a signature in November 1952.

AFSA, and subsequently NSA, were tenants at both the Naval Security Station and Arlington Hall Station, with by far the larger component located at AHS. This tenant status created management and personnel problems, but as early as 1951 plans were laid for a new headquarters.

The original selection was Fort Knox, Kentucky, but this occasioned severe civilian dissatisfaction, and a hastily convened committee then selected Fort Meade, Maryland, about twenty-five miles from the center of Washington, D.C. The selection of Fort Meade was a compromise between the need to remove the new headquarters from potential atomic bomb blast damage and the reluctance of the cryptologic workforce to move to more remote locations. The move to Fort Meade occurred in stages, beginning with an interim move of advance elements to buildings that later became the military barracks, in 1955. The move was completed in 1957 with the opening of OPS1, a three-story structure. An additional, nine-story building was added in 1963.

The communications security components remained at the Ward Circle Naval Security Station until their own building was constructed on Fort Meade in 1968. Owing to rapid growth in the 1950s, the original building was too small even before NSA moved to Fort Meade in 1957. Desperate for more floor space, NSA began renting buildings at a new technical park being built outside what was then known as Friendship Airport (now Baltimore-Washington International). The facility quickly became known as FANX — Friendship Annex.

George A. Brownell

"COMINT is a national responsibility (as distinct from the responsibility of any particular Service, department or agency) and that as a consequence the activity must be so managed and organized as to exploit all available intelligence resources in the participating departments and agencies in order to obtain the optimum results for each and for the Government as a whole."

Brownell Committee Report

"The communications intelligence activities of the United States are a national responsibility."

Harry S. Truman
October 27, 1952

As part of his attempt to unify the cryptologic business, the Secretary of Defense appointed Major General (later Lieutenant General) Ralph Canine, a no-nonsense former artillery officer for General George Patton, as NSA's first director. It was practically Canine's first exposure to intelligence, but he brought to the task a willingness to make tough decisions and a determination to force unification on the reluctant cryptologic services. General Canine presided over the greatest expansion of American cryptologic assets ever, both human and machine. He spurred research and development into the new field of computers, he began work on the fastest and most reliable communications network in the federal government, and he pushed the expansion of field sites (the number of field sites grew from 42 in 1952 to over 90 by 1956, Canine's final year at NSA). Most of all, Canine cultivated a highly professional workforce; he enhanced internal training opportunities, began sending senior executives for external education, and strove to promote high performers to the most senior Civil Service grades.

The United States and the Soviet Union were allies during World War II, but the spirit of harmony fostered by their victory over Nazi Germany lasted only a short time. The problems and rivalry encountered in seeking to settle the residual problems of seven years of war were only a harbinger of things to come. It soon became clear that the U.S. and USSR, as leaders of their respective blocs, were engaged in a new kind of conflict. A "cold war" began in the late 1940s, and it threatened to become actual combat at any time, a new war that could involve nuclear weapons. The USSR detonated its first atomic weapon in 1949, years ahead of American estimates. In the 1950s, Soviet advances in rocket science increased the possibility that the continental United States could become a nuclear battleground. However, little was known with certainty about the post-World War II Soviet military, and obtaining reliable information about the country or its military capabilities was difficult, if not impossible, through conventional intelligence methods.

Soon after World War II ended, SIGINT provided evidence to the United States that the Soviet Union had inimical intentions. In 1946, cryptanalysts solved a system used by the Soviet espionage services during wartime, and, by reading about 2,000 espionage-related messages, learned that the USSR had penetrated many civil and military organizations during the war, including the White House, Treasury Department, Office of Strategic Services (predecessor of the CIA), and the Manhattan Project, which developed the atomic bomb. This secret information was passed to the FBI and resulted in the investigation of some Americans for espionage and the elimination of a number of espionage rings.

"I think, at the time NSA was formed, if the Director of NSA had not been as strong and foreseeing an individual as General Canine, we might have had to go through another reorganization [and] the [whole] thing might have fallen."

Solomon Kullback

LTG Ralph J. Canine, USA

Noted for his on-the-spot inspections, General Ralph Canine, the first director of NSA, once visited the Naval Security Station on Nebraska Avenue in Washington, D.C., "just to see what went on there." It was a hot, humid morning in July 1953, and one of the rooms General Canine looked in had only a window and a transom for ventilation. A transom fan had been requested, but delivery had not yet been made. As General Canine walked into the room, he asked the all-female group how they were doing. One of the women, who had never learned to recognize military rank insignia, bluntly responded, "We'd be doing a helluva lot better, Sergeant, if we could get someone to put a fan in that transom." Everyone in the room, including the military supervisor, sat in stunned silence, awaiting a display of indignation from General Canine, but it never came. He just smiled, sympathized with the plight of the workers, and left, saying, "I'll see what I can do about it." He never let on who he was. As soon as the general had departed, the woman was given quick instruction on military ranks — and within a few minutes a crew arrived to install the transom fan.

The Air Force aircraft for COMINT reconnaissance in the 1950s

In the late 1950s, the Air Force switched to the McDonnell Douglas RC-130

President Dwight D. Eisenhower, concerned about Soviet strategic capabilities, cast about for information regarding this threat. Until CIA U-2s began flying in 1956, virtually nothing definite was available about the USSR except from SIGINT. In fact, a panel in 1954 judged that 90 percent of America's warning information would come from SIGINT. Under the Eisenhower administration, NSA began expanding and enhancing its capabilities. Worried about timely warning, the president supported development of communications for critical information. In the early 1950s, SIGINT sites began sprouting up in Europe to warn the U.S. and NATO of a possible Soviet attack.

As one facet of the energized collection effort, a program of aerial reconnaissance around the periphery of the Soviet Union was begun in the 1940s and expanded in the 1950s, carried out by the U.S. Air Force and the Navy. In the postwar period, the services at first used standard military aircraft, such as B-17s, for these flights. A converted B-29 bomber, the RB-50, served as the first strategic COMINT collection platform. Increasingly, the services outfitted reconnaissance versions of other military aircraft —
the C-130, for example, became the RC-130 for reconnaissance purposes. This was a dangerous but necessary activity; during the Cold War period of 1945-1977, a total of more than 40 reconnaissance aircraft were shot down. Of the 152 cryptologists who lost their lives since World War II, 64 were engaged in aerial reconnaissance. For example, on September 2, 1958, an RC-130 on its initial flight out of Adana, Turkey, strayed over the border into Soviet Armenia and was shot down with the loss of all seventeen airmen aboard. It became one of the most celebrated incidents of the Cold War. As need required, aerial reconnaissance was conducted in other areas of the world, including support to American forces in the Vietnam War. Some of these flights also resulted in downed aircraft and loss of life, e.g., the shootdown of the Navy EC-121 in the Sea of Japan on April 15, 1969, and loss of Army aircraft in Indochina.

EC - 121

Securing U.S. Communications

In the 1950s, NSA pioneered new point-to-point communications security. The KW-26, adopted throughout the Defense Department, was composed partly of tubes and partly of solid state electronics. It was used wherever the U.S. needed the high-grade cryptography at large, fixed-site communications centers. By the time NSA designed a successor to the KW-26, cryptography had gone entirely to solid state designs. The KG-84, much lighter and easier to maintain than earlier cryptography, was first deployed in the 1980s to communications centers around the world.

The most successful voice system through the 1960s was the KY-3, developed by Bell Laboratories to replace existing, and marginally adequate, voice security systems. Using wideband technology, the KY-3 offered high-

KW-26

Adlai Stevenson, UN ambassador during the Kennedy/Johnson administration, using the KY-3 (device is in the cabinet).
Inset photo shows a KY-3.

quality secure voice with excellent security. It was eventually teamed with other equipment into the Autosevocom worldwide secure voice system. But the crypto gear resided in a safe, and the initial expense limited the number of users. Developed for battlefield use, the Vinson (KY-57/58) equipment was smaller and lighter than earlier voice encryption. It was the first secure unit that could be remotely keyed, an important capability in wartime, when units using secure voice systems could be overrun. Voice encryption continued to represent the biggest problem in information security. The known Soviet exploitation of U.S.

unenciphered telephone calls in the 1970s spurred the search for a small, cheap, user-friendly secure telephone. NSA engineers developed a public key algorithm and mated it with a desk telephone — the STU-III. It did away with the requirement for a safe full of equipment, needed only annual rekeying, cost only $2,000 per set, and was made by three commercial contractors. Hundreds of thousands of units were manufactured. The STU-III proved itself as a vital security device for the military during Operations DESERT SHIELD and DESERT STORM.

President Ronald Reagan using a STU-III

The Cuban Missile Crisis

A U-2 flight on October 14, 1962, discovered the presence of Soviet offensive nuclear missiles in Cuba. Although photography provided the early information, all intelligence sources, including SIGINT, were tasked to find more information. NSA's most effective response was to send a SIGINT collection vessel, the Oxford, to Cuban waters to monitor Cuban and Soviet communications. During the tense moments following President Kennedy's imposition of a naval quarantine around Cuba, SIGINT provided the first indication that Soviet vessels had stopped in the mid-Atlantic, awaiting further instructions. It was the first clue that the Soviets might not challenge the American forces arrayed around the island. SIGINT also provided indications when the Soviets ended the period of crisis. Although photographic intelligence raised the initial warning, SIGINT provided much of the operational intelligence to President Kennedy and other military and civilian decision-makers during the crisis.

Soviet strategic missile sites under construction in Cuba

The *Oxford*, a Navy COMINT collection vessel

As in America's previous wars, U.S. SIGINT capabilities supported American troops during combat operations in the field during the Vietnam War — but not without tragic losses. Davis Station, first occupied in 1961, was named for SP4 James T. Davis, who arrived with the first Army Security Agency (ASA) contingent to Vietnam. Davis was on a direction finding (DF) mission when his truck was ambushed by Viet Cong south of Saigon. Ten of the eleven on the truck, including Davis, were killed. Davis was the first American serviceman killed in action during the Vietnam conflict.

RU-21 aircraft, used by ASA for ARDF

Airborne radio direction finding (ARDF) was the most successful SIGINT technique used during the war. It became a primary targeting tool for American forces. The first ARDF aircraft was introduced into the country by the ASA in 1962 as a way to lessen the danger of DF missions like the one that Davis had been on. Designed by an Army engineer, it was rushed to Vietnam and became an instant success.

The Air Force entered the ARDF business with a converted C-47. Originally called PHYLLIS ANN, the Air Force program did not become operational until 1966, but eventually provided a rapid fix capability.

Entrance to ASA's first station, Davis Station, located outside Saigon

The ARDF program endured its share of losses: two Army helicopters, one RU-21 twin-engine ARDF aircraft, and six Air Force EC-47s went down in Vietnam. U.S. Marine Corps SIGINT personnel supported the forces marooned by enemy fire at Khe Sanh during the winter and spring of 1968. Throughout the war, tactical SIGINT was a critical intelligence resource.

The Air Force ARDF platform: an EC-47

Vietnam was not the last war in which cryptology supported American forces. In a visit to NSA after DESERT STORM, the desert campaign to liberate Kuwait from Iraqi aggression, President George Bush expressed his appreciation for cryptologic support. He called the dedicated cryptologists "unsung heroes." Although the story of American cryptology has had to remain secret for decades, the ability to protect U.S. official communications and the ability to exploit the communications of enemies or potential enemies helped keep the United States out of war, shortened the time of war when combat was inevitable, and saved tens of thousands of American and Allied lives.

A Marine COMINT unit at
Khe Sanh (under fire)

"...the 509th Radio Research Group (an element of the Army Security Agency)...provided outstanding support in intercepting and interpreting enemy radio communications during the Vietnam conflict."

General Bruce Palmer, Jr., USA

NSA & Its People

The efforts of NSA's Research & Engineering organization have significantly advanced the state of the art in both the scientific and business worlds.

Military and civilian personnel in the National Security Operations Center work around the clock to keep U.S. decision-makers informed about significant developments affecting the national interest.

Thanks to the people in the Special Processing Laboratory, NSA has made ground-breaking developments in semiconductor technology.

Most NSA employees, both civilian and military, are headquartered at Fort George G. Meade, Maryland, approximately halfway between Washington and Baltimore. NSA's workforce represents an unusual combination of specialties, including analysts, engineers, physicists, mathematicians, linguists, computer scientists, researchers, customer relations specialists, security officers, data flow experts, managers, and administrative and clerical assistants, to name just a few.

It is said that NSA is the largest employer of mathematicians in the United States and perhaps the world. Mathematicians at NSA contribute directly to the two missions of the Agency: some help design cipher systems that will protect the integrity of U.S. information systems, while others search for weaknesses in adversaries' codes.

Technology and the world change rapidly, and NSA places great emphasis on its employees' staying ahead of these changes by providing employee training and development programs. The National Cryptologic School addresses the professional and technical development of NSA employees and provides the unique training needed by both the NSA work force and several elements throughout the Department of Defense. NSA sponsors employees for bachelor and graduate-level study at the Nation's top universities and colleges; selected Agency employees attend the various war colleges of the U.S. Armed Forces.

"...the skills and competence of [NSA employees] are second to none...forward thinking innovativeness and willingness to take risks keep us at the forefront of our business."

from the "National Cryptologic Strategy for the 21st Century"

The NSA and Technology

About the time of World War I, commercial and government inventors began experimenting with and developing electro-mechanical machines to encipher and decipher messages. All major combatants in World War II adopted sophisticated cipher machines for at least some of their communications. Great Britain and the United States developed machines of increasing power and complexity for solving their enemies' cryptomachine systems.

When the German military adopted the ENIGMA, a high-grade cipher machine, the Polish Cipher Bureau invented a cryptanalytic machine, codenamed the Bombe, to aid cryptanalysis. The British and U.S. cryptanalysts made adaptations to the Bombe, and used banks of Bombes to good effect against the German Navy.

The Germans had cipher devices even more sophisticated than the ENIGMA. The TUNNY was one such high-grade cryptomachine. In 1943, capitalizing on human error in the use of TUNNY, British cryptanalysts solved the system in theory. In practice, individual TUNNY messages required too much processing time for use in military operations. To enable timely exploitation, British engineers and cryptanalysts invented a device known as COLOSSUS, which had many characteristics associated with modern computers.

By 1945, U.S. Army and Navy cryptologists had considerable experience devising or using special-purpose computing devices. The challenge was to transfer that knowledge to the design of a general-purpose computer capable of multiple applications. The Army and Navy continued in-house and outside research to develop computers. This dual research track continued as American cryptology was centralized under the National Security Agency.

By late 1950, government and industry working together produced the general-purpose computer ATLAS. The ATLAS and subsequent computing systems used innovative input and storage devices — drum storage, then later tape drives; transistor technology; remote job access; and chip technology.

NSA and a contractor developed a system, nicknamed HARVEST, that remained in service from 1962 to 1976, a long time-span for a computer system. HARVEST proved to be difficult to program and slower than planned, but its development and use was a profitable experience for those involved in developing future generations of computers.

Today, NSA conducts one of the U.S. Government's leading research and development programs. The Agency's R&D projects have significantly advanced the state of the art in the scientific and business worlds. Early interest in cryptanalytic research led to the first large-scale computer and the first solid-state computer, predecessors to the modern computer. NSA pioneered efforts in flexible storage capabilities, which led to the development of the tape cassette. The Agency also made ground-breaking developments in semiconductor technology, developed the first optical "transistor," and was involved in early face recognition technology.

NSA remains a world leader in many technology fields, employing that technological advantage to protect our data and communications while providing our Nation's leaders with critical intelligence information.

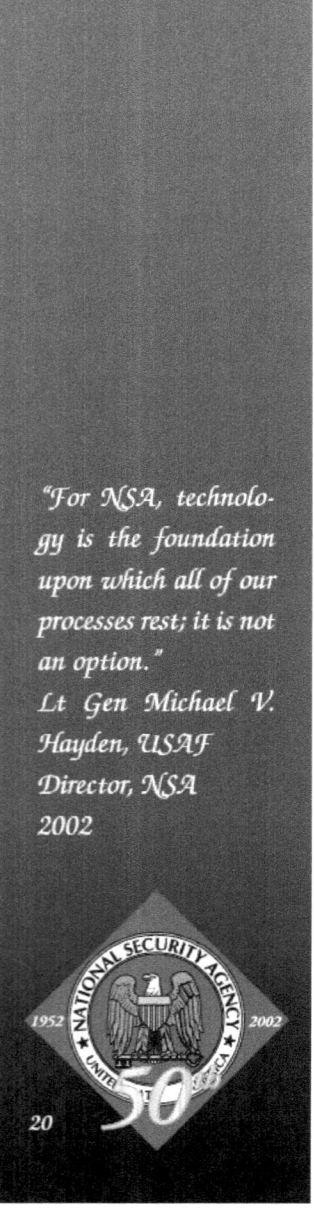

"For NSA, technology is the foundation upon which all of our processes rest; it is not an option."
Lt Gen Michael V. Hayden, USAF
Director, NSA
2002

Central Security Service

The Central Security Service (CSS) was established by Presidential Directive in 1972 to promote a full partnership between NSA and the cryptologic elements of the Armed Forces, or service cryptologic elements (SCEs). By combining NSA and CSS, a more unified Department of Defense cryptologic effort emerged. The Director of NSA is also the Chief of the CSS, and he is assisted in this role by his Deputy, CSS, a Major General or Rear Admiral (upper half). The CSS also includes a jointly staffed headquarters. Army, Navy and Marine Corps, Air Force, and Coast Guard operating elements, and such other subordinate elements and

facilities as may be assigned to the CSS by the Secretary of Defense. The SCEs are the U.S. Army Intelligence and Security Command (INSCOM); the Naval Security Group Command (NAVSECGRU or NSG), including the Marine Support Battalion; the Air Intelligence Agency (AIA); and the Coast Guard Intelligence Directorate. The SCEs, on behalf of their services, are both consumers and producers of intelligence information. They advocate cryptologic requirements of their services within the crytologic enterprise, and they provide forces and capabilities to NSA/CSS organizations at NSA headquarters and in the field. The SCEs also provide tactical units and personnel assigned to military commands. These units and personnel directly support and take tasking from their commanders, but rely on the SCE headquarters for technical support and other assistance. The CSS and SCEs originally focused on SIGINT but now have responsibilities in Information Assurance as well.

"Our relationship with the Service Cryptologic Elements is essential. We cannot accomplish our part in this Nation's defense unless it is close, continual, and effective."

Lt Gen Michael V. Hayden, USAF Director, NSA 1999

Remembering Those Who Made the Ultimate Sacrifice

The National Security Agency/Central Security Service Cryptologic Memorial is intended to honor and remember those who have given their lives, "serving in silence," in the line of duty since World War II. The names listed include Army, Navy, Air Force, Marine, and civilian cryptologists who have made the ultimate sacrifice in hostile action, under fire in peacetime activities, and in other tragedies. It is hoped that this memorial will serve as an important reminder both of the crucial role that cryptology plays in keeping the United States secure and of the courage of these individuals to carry out their mission at such a dear price.

The memorial is a black granite wall, 12 feet wide and 8 feet high, centered with a triangle. The words THEY SERVED IN SILENCE, etched into the polished stone at the cap of the triangle, recognize that cryptologic service has always been a silent service — secretive by its very nature. Below these words, the NSA seal and the names of the 152 military and civilian cryptologists who have given their lives in service to their country are carved into the granite. The names are at the base of the triangle because these cryptologists and their ideals — dedication to mission, dedication to workmate, and dedication to country — form the foundation for cryptologic service.

The striking memorial was designed by an NSA employee. It is housed in the NSA Headquarters complex at Fort Meade, MD. A replica of the memorial is on display at the National Cryptologic Museum.

"For without belittling the courage with which men have died, we should not forget those acts of courage with which men have lived."

John F. Kennedy

Adjacent to the National Cryptologic Museum and accessible by a modest walking path is the National Vigilance Park. Dedicated on September 2, 1997, the park and its Aerial Reconnaissance Memorial stand to honor those "silent warriors" who risked their lives performing airborne signals intelligence missions during the Cold War.

The centerpiece of the memorial is a C-130 aircraft, refurbished to resemble the reconnaissance-configured RC-130 that was downed by Soviet fighters over Soviet Armenia on September 2, 1958. The backdrop for the aircraft is a semi-circle of 18 trees, each representing the various types of aircraft downed during U.S. aerial reconnaissance missions.

Rounding out the park is an RU-8D Seminole, paying tribute to the service and sacrifice of Army soldiers assigned to perform aerial reconnaissance and cryptologic intelligence gathering missions during the Vietnam War.

The National Cryptologic Museum

Located at NSA Headquarters, Ft. George G. Meade, Maryland, the National Cryptologic Museum collection contains thousands of artifacts that collectively serve to sustain the history of the cryptologic profession. Ranging from rare books hundreds of years old to computers that are barely obsolete, the collection neglects no aspect of cryptology.

Because many cryptologic principles are timeless, many of the earliest and most important artifacts now held by the museum were originally obtained as training aids. The rare books mentioned above are an excellent example. Although dating back as early as 1518, these books bear library circulation marks that show that they were part of the Signals Intelligence Service library prior to World War II. Other artifacts, such as the 1930s-vintage Hebern machine, were acquired to test their security for possible use in United States military and diplomatic correspondence.

World War II saw dramatic increases in the use of machines in all aspects of cryptology. Many of these are also an integral part of the Agency's collection. One example, the now famous German ENIGMA, stands as a silent reminder of the consequences of poor communications security. At the same time, the machine used to read the equally well-known Japanese PURPLE cipher clearly illustrates the resourcefulness of American cryptanalysts.

Following World War II, a concerted effort was made from around the world. The intent was to provide a base of study for engineers of the Armed Forces Security Agency (NSA's forerunner) in the development in the next generation of cryptologic machinery. This was done, and thanks to the foresight of some of those involved, a true museum collection was born. Today, the National Cryptologic Museum continues the dual role of educating the work force and documenting America's cryptologic heritage.

The National Cryptologic Museum is located on Colony 7 Road just off Maryland Route 32 and adjacent to the Baltimore-Washington Parkway. The museum is open to the public; school groups and civic organizations are welcome. Appointments are required for large groups or for special occasions.

For more information, call the museum at 301-688-5849.

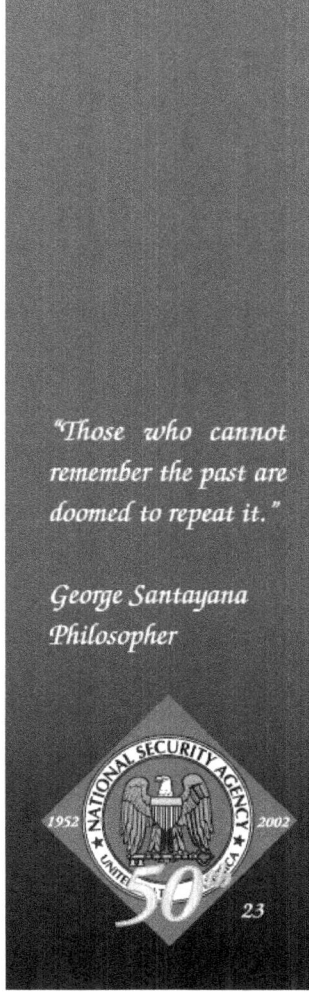

"Those who cannot remember the past are doomed to repeat it."

George Santayana
Philosopher

In 1965, LTG Marshall S. Carter, USA, Director NSA, directed a device be designed to represent the National Security Agency.

The device created is described as: an insignia which shall be a circle bordered white. In the chief semicircle border, the words National Security Agency. In the base semicircle border, the words United States of America, separated on either side by a five pointed star, silver; in a field, blue, an American eagle displayed, wings inverted, all proper. The dexter and sinister talons clutching a key, silver. On the breast of the eagle, the escutcheon, chief blue, supported by paleways of thirteen pieces red and white.

In heraldry, the eagle is a symbol of courage, supreme power, and authority. Use of the eagle in the NSA insignia symbolizes the national scope of the mission of the Agency. The escutcheon, or shield, placed on the breast of the eagle is a very ancient mode of bearing. A description of the escutcheon, taken from that of the Great Seal of the United States, explains that "the escutcheon is composed of the chief and pale, the two most honorable ordinaries (common figures). The pieces, paly, represent the several states all joined in one solid compact entire, supporting a chief, which unites the whole and represents Congress." The key in the eagle's talons, representing the key to security, evolves from the emblem of St. Peter the Apostle, and his power to loose and to bind. The shape of the insignia, a circle, represents perpetuity of its continuance, the symbol of eternity.